Who F*rted?

LONG SHADOW BOOKS
PUBLISHED BY POCKET BOOKS NEW YORK

Another *Original* publication of LONG SHADOW BOOKS

A Long Shadow Book published by
POCKET BOOKS, a division of Simon & Schuster, Inc.
1230 Avenue of Americas, New York, N.Y. 10020

ISBN: 0-671-50674-9

First Long Shadow Books printing February, 1984

10 9 8 7 6 5 4 3 2

LONG SHADOW BOOKS and colophon are trademarks
of Simon & Schuster, Inc.

Printed in the U.S.A.

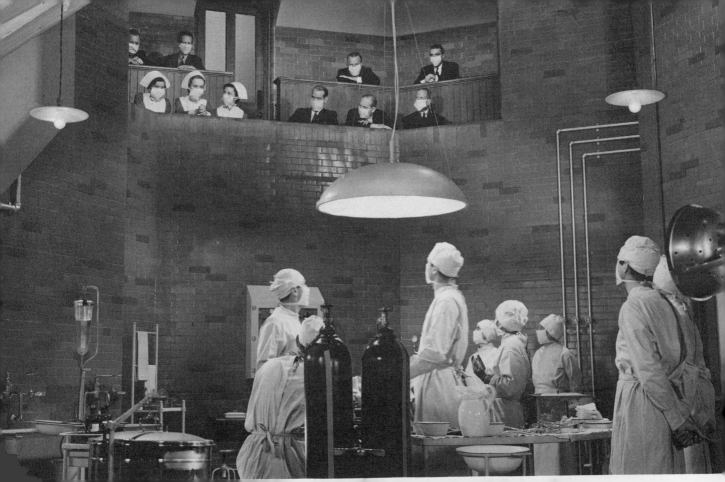